CW01660254

‘God speaks today just as He did before.’

Signs of the Living God

Hazrat Mirza Bashir-ud-Din Mahmud Ahmad[ra] (1889-1965), the Musleh Mau'ud (the Promised Reformer), was the son of the Promised Messiah[as] and his second successor. He was elected as the khalifa of the Ahmadiyya Muslim Community in 1914 at the age of 25 and led the movement for 52 years. In the period of his khilafat, the message of Ahmadiyyat spread to countries as far and wide as the United States of America and Japan. He also set the foundations of the community's administrative structure and launched numerous initiatives for the propagation of Islam, most notably Tehrik-e-Jadid and Waqf-e-Jadid. A prolific writer, orator and the author of a ten-volume commentary of the Holy Qur'an, he leaves a profound and enduring legacy which lasts to the present day.

Signs of the Living God

Hazrat Mirza Bashir-ud-Din Mahmud Ahmad
Khalifatul-Masih II

TRANSLATED BY
THE FAZLE UMAR FOUNDATION

FAZLE UMAR
FOUNDATION

Signs of the Living God

By Hazrat Mirza Bashir-ud-Din Mahmud Ahmad
Khalifatul-Masih II

Present English Edition: UK 2018

FAZLE UMAR
FOUNDATION

Published by:

Islam International Publications Ltd
Unit 3, Bourne Mill Business Park,
Guildford Road, Farnham, Surrey UK, GU9 9PS
United Kingdom

Printed by CPI Group (UK) Ltd, Croydon CR0 4YY

ISBN: 978-1-84880-914-7

Contents

Note

The words in the text in regular brackets ( ) and in between the long dashes—are the words of the author and if any explanatory words or phrases are added by the translator for the purpose of clarification, they have been placed in square brackets [ ].

The name of Muhammad[sa], the Holy Prophet of Islam, has been followed by the abbreviation [sa], which is an abbreviation for the salutation *Sallallahu 'Alaihi Wasallam* (may peace and blessings of Allah be upon him). The names of other prophets and messengers are followed by the abbreviation [as], an abbreviation for *'Alaihis-Salam* (on whom be peace). The actual salutations have not generally been set out in full, but they should nevertheless be understood as being repeated in full in each case. The abbreviation [ra] is used with the names of the companions of the Holy Prophet[sa] and those of the Promised Messiah[as]. It stands for *Radi Allahu 'anhu, 'anha, 'anhum* (may Allah be pleased with him, with her, with them). The abbreviation [rh] stands for *Rahimahullahu Ta'ala* (may Allah have mercy on him). The abbreviation [at] stands for *Ayyadahullahu Ta'ala* (may Allah, the Mighty help him).

Because of their frequency of use and for ease of reading, Islamic terms such as *hadith* or *umma* have, for the most part, not been italicised or transliterated in the main body of the text. Anyone interested in the correct pronunciation of these words can refer to the glossary at the end of the book.

All English renditions of the verses of the Holy Qur'an have been taken from the 2004 edition of Maulawi Sher Ali's translation.

Acknowledgements

First and foremost, gratitude is due to Allah Whose beneficence and mercy blesses all our endeavours. Thereafter, this work would not have been possible without the constant guidance and support of Hazrat Khalifatul Masih V (may Allah be his helper) whose instructions, directives and close attention to detail are a source of help and encouragement to us all.

Heartfelt thanks to Mirza Usman Ahmad for his translation of these two essays and for his efforts in overseeing the project as a whole. I am further thankful to Haseeb Ahmad, Awais Rabbani, Tanwir Mujtaba and Farhan Iqbal for all of their editorial assistance. Finally, mention must be made of Arsalan Qamar, Syed Talib Mehmood and the team at the Review of Religions for all their technical and design support.

Nasir Ahmad Shams
Secretary Fazle Umar Foundation

Foreword

Revelation is a central feature of almost all religions and can be defined as the disclosure of a hidden or future truth by God or other form of deity. All the major religions of the world today testify to the truth of revelation and present prophecies from their scripture as evidence of their divine origins and authenticity.

This is also true of the Islamic tradition which holds that since the time of the Prophet Adam[as], God has revealed Himself to certain individuals and sent them as prophets and messengers to mankind, so that they may guide people and bring them towards the worship of their creator.

In the Holy Qur'an, God says to the Prophet Muhammad[sa]:

وَمَآ اَرْسَلْنٰكَ اِلَّا كَآفَّةً لِّلنَّاسِ بَشِيْرًا وَّنَذِيْرًا وَّلٰكِنَّ اَكْثَرَ النَّاسِ
لَا يَعْلَمُوْنَ۝[1]

[1] *Surah Saba'*, 34:29 [Publishers]

And We have not sent thee but as a bearer of glad tidings and a Warner, for all mankind, but most men know not.

Then with regards to prophecy and revelation God says:

عَٰلِمُ ٱلْغَيْبِ فَلَا يُظْهِرُ عَلَىٰ غَيْبِهِۦٓ أَحَدًا ۝ إِلَّا مَنِ ٱرْتَضَىٰ مِن رَّسُولٍ
فَإِنَّهُۥ يَسْلُكُ مِنۢ بَيْنِ يَدَيْهِ وَمِنْ خَلْفِهِۦ رَصَدًا ۝ لِّيَعْلَمَ أَن قَدْ أَبْلَغُوا۟
رِسَٰلَٰتِ رَبِّهِمْ ۝[2]

He *is the* knower of the unseen; and He reveals not His secrets to anyone, except to him whom He choose, namely a Messenger *of His*. And then He causes an escort *of guarding angels* to go before him and behind him, that He may know that they (His Messengers) have delivered the Messages of their Lord.

When reading these verses together, one can define the Islamic concept of prophecy and revelation as *the divine disclosure of certain hidden truths by God to His messengers in order to establish both the truth of His existence and the veracity of their prophetic claim.* These secrets which God reveals can be events of the

[2] *Surah Al-Jinn*, 72:27-29 [Publishers]

past, present or future which are as yet unknown or forms of knowledge, whether scientific, historical, archaeological or otherwise, which have not yet come to light.

In the following two essays, Hazrat Mirza Bashir-ud-Din Mahmud Ahmad[ra] draws on this criteria to show that like the prophets of the past, Hazrat Mirza Ghulam Ahmad the founder of the Ahmadiyya Muslim Community and the Promised Messiah and Imam Mahdi[as] received news of the unseen from God and these revelations which span across the entire prophetic spectrum found fulfilment at their appointed time. Among the prophecies he mentions are those relating to the future success promised to the Promised Messiah and his community, prophecies regarding natural disasters, particularly those relating to earthquakes, and Hazrat Mirza Ghulam Ahmad's[as] foretelling of the death of John Alexander Dowie, an American evangelist who contemptuously challenged his claims.

Mostly, however, Huzoor turns to the Promised Messiah's[as] prophecies regarding the outbreak of the First World War and the subsequent fall of the Tsar of Russia and shows in intricate detail how each facet of these prophecies was fulfilled in absolute terms. These signs and many others, Huzoor argues, leave no doubt about the truth of the Promised Messiah's[as] claim and show that just as God raised messengers in the past, He has also raised one in this age.

These essays were originally published in Urdu under the titles زندہ خدا کے زبردست نشان (*Zinda Khuda ke Zabardast Nishan*) and خدا کے قہری نشان (*Khuda ke Qehri Nishan*) and can be found in Volume III of *Anwar-ul-'Uloom*.

Signs of the Living God

بِسۡمِ اللّٰہِ الرَّحۡمٰنِ الرَّحِیۡمِ نَحۡمَدُہٗ وَنُصَلِّیۡ عَلٰی رَسُوۡلِہِ الۡکَرِیۡمِ [3]

وَمَا کَانَ رَبُّکَ مُہۡلِکَ الۡقُرٰی حَتّٰی یَبۡعَثَ فِیۡۤ اُمِّہَا رَسُوۡلًا یَّتۡلُوۡا عَلَیۡہِمۡ اٰیٰتِنَا ۚ

وَمَا کُنَّا مُہۡلِکِی الۡقُرٰۤی اِلَّا وَاَہۡلُہَا ظٰلِمُوۡنَ ۝ [4]

Mighty Signs of the Living God

دنیا میں ایک نذیر آیا پر دنیا نے اس کو قبول نہ کیا۔ لیکن خدا اُسے قبول کرے گا اور بڑے زورآور حملوں سے اُس کی سچائی ظاہر کردے گا۔

A Warner came unto the world, but the world accepted him not; yet God shall manifest His favour and demonstrate his truth with powerful assaults.[5]

Twelve years ago a Prophet of India foretold the pitiable plight of the Tsar of Russia.

According to the eternal law of God Almighty, when the world forgets God and falls prey to sin and iniquity; when the morals of people are corrupted and their spirits are low; when the throats of those who hanker

[3] In the name of Allah, the Gracious the Merciful. We praise Allah, the Exalted, the Greatest, and we invoke His blessings on His Holy Messenger[sa]. [Publishers]

[4] And thy Lord would never destroy the towns until He has raised in the mother *town* thereof a Messenger, reciting unto them Our Signs; nor would We destroy the towns unless the people thereof are wrongdoers. *Surah Al-Qasas, 28:60* [Publishers]

[5] *Tadhkirah*, p. 128, 2009 Ed. [Publishers]

for spiritual water are made so dry they ache as though pricked by thorns; when their lips are parched and their eyes sink with the extremities of thirst; God raises a prophet for their guidance and a messenger for their reformation. These [messengers] come as clouds of spiritual water which inundate every swathe of land capable of absorbing their rain and assuage the yearning of the thirsty. They are a light by which those who are shrouded in darkness begin to see. They are a fire which burns the enemies of truth to ashes. They are a jolt of electricity which, by sudden bursts, strikes such power into the fortunate that the blind are able to see, the infirm are able to walk and the mute are able to speak. Their friendship is an antidote to all toxins and enmity to them is such a fatal poison that once it is consumed there are no humanly means or cures that can save people from destruction.

In the present age, the estrangement of people from spirituality, the spread of vice and the prevalence of sin all signify that if God had raised prophets in the past, He must also raise one now, and if a reformer had appeared at any point in history, one must also appear today. The prophecies of earlier prophets unanimously testify that this would be a time for the advent of a prophet. Although there are thousands of differences between the various religions, to the extent that it is difficult to find even a single issue on which they are agreed, yet still they are united in the belief that a prophet is to appear in the latter days. The signs mentioned for his advent are all being fulfilled in this age. Unfortunately, despite the circumstances, need of the age and the combined testimony of all religions, people have made little effort to recognise the prophet of this time whom Allah the Exalted has sent from the heavens just when he was most required. Instead, it seems the world awaits a prophet who will descend from on high flanked by angels, and for whom God Almighty will testify with a thunderous voice that will be heard at once throughout the world; a prophet who has paradise to his right and hell to his left, and who has the power of fate and destiny in his hands. If this is the case, this desire will never be fulfilled. No such prophet has come before, nor will such a prophet appear in the future. It is always human beings who are sent as messengers for the guidance of their fellow people. One species cannot serve as a model for another, whereas the prophets come into the world as exemplars for others. They do not descend from heaven, rather they are born on earth from the wombs of their mothers just like any other human being. A prophet who does not follow in the abiding practice of his predecessors can never appear. Whosoever comes as a prophet will do so in accordance with the precedents set by his antecedents.

I call on those who would listen and see and those who are bestowed with erudition that they ought to know that in accordance with the eternal practice of Allah, which was manifested in the time of the previous prophets, the prophet who was promised in this age has appeared—that is, he who had been foretold to come among the Hindus as Krishna, as Maitreya in Buddhism, and the Promised Messiah in Judaism, Christianity, and Islam. God has shown the same signs for him which He manifested in the past at the hands of the previous prophets. He (the Promised Messiah[as]) also prayed and God Almighty heard his prayers. Through him, those who found no cure for themselves in medicine were healed. That which he foretold and published throughout the world ahead of time was fulfilled exactly, even though none except the messengers of God are given such numerous divine signs. And this is attested to by all religions. The Holy Qur'an says:

فَلَا يُظْهِرُ عَلٰى غَيْبِهٖٓ اَحَدًا ○ اِلَّا مَنِ ارْتَضٰى مِنْ رَّسُوْلٍ[6]

And He reveals not His secrets to anyone.

[6] *Surah Al-Jinn*, 72:27-28 [Publishers]

> Except to him whom He chooses, namely a Messenger *of His*.

Similarly, the Bible says:

> If a prophet speaks in the name of the Lord but the thing does not take place or prove true, it is a word that the Lord has not spoken. The prophet has spoken it presumptuously; do not be frightened by it.[7]

I ask those who seek and enquire after the truth how I can make them understand that the promises found in various religions concerning the Promised Messiah, Mahdi, Krishan, Maitreya, Buddha [and so on] have found their fulfilment in the person of Hazrat Mirza Ghulam Ahmad Qadiani[as], the founder of the Ahmadiyya Community. No one else will be the subject of these prophecies from now until the Day of Judgment. How can I instil your hearts with the knowledge that to recognise the chosen ones of God is a divine blessing against which all worldly accolades pale into insignificance? How can I explain to you that those who fight with God always meet a tragic end and those who reject divine messengers reject God

[7] *Deuteronomy*, New Revised Standard Version, 18:22 [Publishers]

Almighty Himself? If only I possessed a *bugle* by which to rouse all those who are asleep in the world from the depths of their slumber, so that they could see the Sun of God has reached its zenith.

Most parts of the world claim to believe in certain prophets of the past. Sadly, however, few reflect on the basis of their belief. Had they given thought to this and ascertained the proofs which support the truth of their prophets, these same signs would have led them to recognise the messenger of the age without any trouble. Regrettably, in our current time, true faith has given way to inherited belief. If the prophets whom different nations believe in were to reappear today, with the same proofs that were given to them at the time of their advent, they too would be met with hostility from their own followers.

يٰحَسْرَةً عَلَى الْعِبَادِ ۚ مَا يَأْتِيْهِمْ مِّنْ رَّسُوْلٍ اِلَّا كَانُوْا بِهٖ يَسْتَهْزِءُوْنَ[8]

> Alas for *My* servants! there comes not a Messenger to them but they mock at him.

God Almighty showed so many proofs and signs for the truth of the Promised Messiah[as] that: کافی ہیں ماننے کو اگر اہل

[8] *Surah Ya Sin*, 36:31 [Publishers]

کوئی ہے[9] 'they are sufficient for those who are ready to accept them.'[10] When the Promised Messiah[as] was unknown in the world he recorded the following revelation on page 241 of his book *Barahin-e-Ahmadiyya Part III* (that was published in 1883 throughout India):

يَأْتِيكَ مِنْ كُلِّ فَجٍّ عَمِيقٍ وَّيَأْتُونَ مِنْ كُلِّ فَجٍّ عَمِيقٍ[11]

> That is, people and gifts will come to you from the far flung places of the world.

Again on page 489 of *Barahin-e-Ahmadiyya Part IV*, published in 1884, he recorded the revelation:

فَحَانَ اَنْ تُعَانَ وَتُعْرَفَ بَيْنَ النَّاسِ[12]

> The time has come that you should be helped and be recognised among people.

Similarly, in a supplement published with the

[9] *Tohfa-e-Golarhviyyah*, *Ruhani Khaza'in* Vol. 17, p. 78 [Publishers]
[10] The original verse as written by the Promised Messiah[as] is: کافی ہے سوچنے کو اگر اہل کوئی ہے. Meaning: 'There is much to ponder for those who are ready to accept.' However, as can be seen above Hazrat Khalifatul Masih II[ra] has quoted the verse slightly differently to its original form. [Publishers]
[11] *Barahin-e-Ahmadiyya Part III*, *Ruhani Khaza'in* Vol. 1, p. 267 [Publishers]
[12] *Barahin-e-Ahmadiyya Part IV*, *Ruhani Khaza'in* Vol. 1, p. 581 [Publishers]

newspaper *Riyaz-e-Hind Amritsar* on 1 March 1886, one of the many revelations recorded in it says:

خدا تیرے نام کو اس روز تک جو دنیا منقطع ہو جائے عزت کے ساتھ قائم
رکھے گا۔اور تیری دعوت کو دنیا کے کناروں تک پہنچا دے گا

God will maintain your name with honour till the day when the world comes to an end and will convey your message to the ends of the earth.[13]

And:

میں تیری تبلیغ کو دنیا کے چاروں کونوں تک پہنچاؤں گا

I shall carry your message to the four corners of the earth.[14]

[In effect through these revelations God says:]

People and gifts will come to you from all four corners of the world. The time has come for your help and renown among the people. God Almighty will spread your teaching across the entire world.

13 *Tadhkirah*, p.181, 2009 Ed. [Publishers]
14 *Tadhkirah*, p.405, 2009 Ed. [Publishers]

Events have shown that these words emanated from Allah the Exalted. For after their manifestation hundreds of thousands of people accepted the Promised Messiah[as] and his name was elevated in Europe, America, Africa, Australia and the entire continent of Asia. Pure souls from every continent accepted his invitation and continue to do so. And despite all opposition, each day his community progresses with ever greater speed.

Again on page 519 of *Barahin-e-Ahmadiyya* he prophesied that plague would break out in India.[15] Almost 15 years later the disease reached the subcontinent. Even now, hundreds of thousands of people die from the disease every year with no end in sight. In the early days when the death toll was contained, the Promised Messiah[as] published an advertisement about a dream in which he saw plants representing the plague being sown all over the Punjab, (it was entitled *Plague* and was written and published on 6 February 1898). Soon after, the plague broke out in the province. He also received the revelation: موتا موتی لگ رہی ہے 'There is death everywhere.' (See *Al-Wasiyyat* published on 27 February 1905, and the newspaper

[15] In the current Urdu edition of *Ruhani Khaza'in* this can be found in Vol.1, p. 620 [Publishers]

Al-Hakm Vol. 9, Issue. 7, p. 11).

Similarly, he foretold news of the earthquake which struck on 4 April 1905, before its occurrence with the words: زلزلہ کا دھکا 'Shock of earthquake' (December 1903). [Again God revealed]:

عَفَتِ الدِّیَارُ مَحِلُّھَا وَ مُقَامُھَا

That is, the earthquake would be so severe it would demolish buildings from their foundations and both temporary residences and permanent ones will be raised from their foundations and collapse. The latter revelation was published a year before the earthquake occurred in the newspaper *Al-Hakm* on 31 May 1904, and *Al-Badr* on 24 May and 1 June 1904. Following this revelation an earthquake duly devastated the Kangra Valley and claimed 30,000 lives. The number of injured was even higher. Whole villages were completely destroyed and the Punjab was convulsed from one end to another. For miles on end, lives and property were destroyed in towns and villages and its tremors were felt outside the Punjab, as far as even Bengal. Never in its history had India seen an earthquake of this magnitude.

Again, at the time of the announcement of the partition of Bengal, all high-ranking government officials were adamant this decision would not be reversed and English ministers consistently made public statements to this effect. In the February 1906 English and Urdu editions of the *Review of Religions*, Vol. 5, Issue 2, as well as the newspapers *Badr*, *Al-Hakm* and the *Indian Mirror Culcutta*, the Promised Messiah[as] published the revelation:

پہلے بنگال کی نسبت جو کچھ حکم جاری کیا گیا تھا،اب ان کی دلجوئی ہوگی

> Relating to the order that had been given concerning Bengal at first, they (i.e., the Bengalis) will be conciliated now.[16]

Accordingly, six years later, despite the intransigence of the [British] rulers, the revocation of the partition was announced at the coronation of King George V and thereby this sign was fulfilled in an extraordinary manner.

Then there is the case of the American John Alexander Dowie, a resident of Chicago and the founder of a large Christian sect who declared himself to be Elijah. On one occasion when Dowie issued a

[16] *Tadhkirah*, p. 791, 2009 Ed. The words of this revelation have been reproduced exactly as they were first published in the February 1906 *Review of Religions* referenced in the main text. [Publisher]

series of poisonous and offensive claims against Islam, the Promised Messiah[as] published a handbill against him and said he would be overtaken by a grievous torment. Subsequently, Dowie's wife and son turned against him and he was shown to be of illegitimate birth. His followers also left him. In the end he was stricken by paralysis and died in a state of madness. There are many signs of this nature, but the reason I have chosen to mention Dowie in particular is because he had acquired particular renown in both Europe and America and his followers were spread across both continents.

The collapse of the Turkish (Ottoman) Empire and Sultan Abdul Hamid Khan's deposition by powerful elements within his own state was also proclaimed by the Promised Messiah[as] ahead of time in an announcement published on 24 May 1897. His words were fulfilled in the most emphatic manner. Likewise, regarding the Iranian [Constitutional] Revolution, he published the following revelation on 15 January 1906: تزلزل در ایوان کسریٰ فتاد. That is: 'The palace of Chosros has been shaken.' (See *Review of Religions* Urdu, January 1906). Three years later this revelation was fulfilled with the Iranian Revolution and the overthrow and exile of the Shah.

The Balkan Wars were also foretold in the revelations of the Promised Messiah[as]. One example is the following revelation published in the Urdu *Review of Religions*, January 1904:

غُلِبَتِ الرُّوْمُ فِيْٓ اَدْنَى الْاَرْضِ وَهُمْ مِّنْۢ بَعْدِ غَلَبِهِمْ سَيَغْلِبُوْنَ

> The Byzantines have been defeated in the land nearby, but after their defeat they will soon be victorious.

Accordingly, the Balkan powers defeated the Turks near Constantinople, which was the capital of Turkey. However, immediately afterwards, due to infighting within the [Balkan alliance], the Turks experienced a great victory [by reoccupying] Adrianople (Edirne). As a result of this, both shades of the prophecy were fulfilled in an extraordinary manner.

Regarding the current war, the Promised Messiah[as] published the following prophecy in 1907:[17]

اک نشاں ہے آنیوالا آج سے کچھ دن کے بعد

جس سے گردش کھائیں گے دیہات و شہر و مرغزار

[17] While this poem was written in 1905, it was first published in 1908 and not in 1907 as appears in the original manuscript. [Publisher]

آئے گا قہر خدا سے خلق پر اک انقلاب
اک برہنہ سے نہ یہ ہوگا کہ تا باندھے ازار
یک بیک اک زلزلہ سے سخت جنبش کھائیں گے[18]
کیا بشر اور کیا شجر اور کیا حجر اور کیا بحار
اک جھپک میں یہ زمیں ہوجائے گی زیروزبر
نالیاں خوں کی چلیں گی جیسے آب رودبار

[18] Divine revelation has repeatedly employed the word earthquake in this context and has indicated that the earthquake will be an example of the Judgment Day. Indeed, it should be termed as 'earthquake of Judgment' which is described in the verse اِذَا زُلۡزِلَتِ الۡاَرۡضُ زِلۡزَالَهَا. But I am not able to apply the word earthquake with certainty upon its actual manifestation. It is possible that it may not be a common earthquake but some other dire calamity, which would be an example of the Judgment Day, the like of which has not been witnessed before, and which would bring about great destruction of life and property. If no such extraordinary sign appears, while people have not openly reformed their way of life, I shall in such case have been proved false. However, as I have already written repeatedly, this severe calamity which God has referred to as an earthquake will not wield its impact because of any religious dispute. Neither can a catastrophe strike against anyone because they are a Hindu or a Christian, nor can it strike because someone has not entered into my allegiance. No one will be affected on account of this reason. Instead, a person who, regardless of their faith, is a habitual wrong-doer and has given over to sinfulness and impiety and is an adulterer; murderous; a thief; unduly submits to ill-thoughts; foul-mouthed and of indecent character ought to fear for themselves. But even then, if they repent they will be spared from grief. And that good deeds and the pious character of people can ward off an affliction is not an immutable decree. *Barahin-e-Ahmadiyya Part V, Ruhani Khaza'in* Vol. 21, p. 151-152

رات جو رکھتے تھے پوشاکیں برنگ یاسمین
صبح کر دے گی انہیں مثل درختان چنار

ہوش اڑ جائیں گے انساں کے پرندوں کے حواس
بھولیں گے نغموں کو اپنے سب کبوتر اور ہزار

ہر مسافر پر وہ ساعت سخت ہے اور وہ گھڑی
راہ کو بھولیں گے ہو کر مست و بے خود راہوار

خون سے مردوں کے کوہستان کے آب رواں
سرخ ہوجائیں گے جیسے ہو شراب انجبار

مضمحل ہوجائیں گے اس خوف سے سب جن و انس
زار بھی ہو گا تو ہوگا اس گھڑی باحال زار

اک نمونہ قہر کا ہوگا وہ ربانی نشان
آسماں حملے کرے گا کھینچ کراپنی کٹار

ہاں نہ کر جلدی سے انکار اے سفیہہ ناشناس
اس پہ ہے میری سچائی کا سبھی دارومدار

وحی حق کی بات ہے ہوکر رہے گی بے خطا
کچھ دنوں کر صبر ہو کر متقی اور بردبار

یہ گماں مت کر کہ یہ سب بدگمانی ہے معاف
قرض ہے واپس ملے گا تجھ کو یہ سارا ادھار

A Sign will appear some days hence.

Which will overwhelm country and town and meadow.

People will be seized in a wave of Divine wrath,

So suddenly that a naked one will have no time to secure his loin cloth.

Suddenly an earthquake will severely shake them all—

Be they humans, trees, rocks or oceans.

In the twinkling of an eye the earth will be turned upside down,

And streams of blood will flow like channel tides.

Those whose night garments were white as jasmine,

Will wake up in the morning as if clad in red like the poplar tree.

Men and animals will go out of their minds

And nightingales and pigeons will forget their songs.

That hour will bear heavily upon every traveller,

And those on a journey will lose their way in agony.

The waters of mountain streams will run red like red wine,

With the blood of the dead.

Men high and low will be convulsed with fear and the Tsar himself will,

At that hour, be in sad case.

That Divine Sign will be a specimen of terror.

Heaven will attack with a drawn sword.

Hasten not to repudiate this, thou stupid fool,

For my truthfulness depends entirely on the fulfilment of this sign.

This is a prophecy based on Divine revelation and will surely be fulfilled;

Wait then a while in righteousness and steadfastness.

Do not presume your ill-thoughts will be forgiven,

It is a debt that will be repaid to you in full.

[According to another revelation of similar effect]: کشتیاں چلتی ہیں تا ہوں کُشتیاں[19]. That is, vessels will sail in abundance from place to place for the sake of fighting. As we can see, seafaring vessels are playing a critical role in the current conflict as they ferry soldiers of various countries to different theatres of war. And this is happening to an extent unparalleled in history. Furthermore, the use of submarines is causing great devastation. Similarly, thousands of large and small ships are constantly being used for naval blockades and their number is 10 times greater than in any previous war. The word *kishti* (ship) [found in the prophecy] though also used for larger vessels, is especially applicable to smaller craft, with reference here to the ruthlessness of [German] U-boats and submarines which have become a significant component of the war at sea.

These signs are just a small selection from thousands of similar other signs that God Almighty has manifested through the Promised Messiah[as]. They

[19] *Tadhkirah*, p. 821, 2009 Ed. [Publishers]

are such that once they have become known, there is no room left to doubt the truth of the claim of the Promised Messiah[as]. For it is impossible for human beings to forecast such numerous and powerful events of the future which then go on to find clear fulfilment at their appointed time.

If these prophecies had been just a few instances one could attribute it to guesswork, but to make thousands of prophecies which find fulfilment at the appointed time is something that is beyond the power of human beings.

The followers of different religions accept the truth of the prophecies of their prophets which are found in their scriptures. Therefore, they assert their truth, even when there is doubt that these prophecies may have been added at a later date. Why then, after the manifestation of such prophecies that are free from all suspicion, are such people not willing to accept the truth of the Promised Messiah[as]?

We live in the age of the printing press and today things are not assumed to be true simply on the basis of spoken testimonies. All the prophecies of the Promised Messiah[as] I have hitherto alluded to were recorded in various books, newspapers, periodicals and essays ahead of time. Therefore, not even our staunchest enemies can claim these prophecies are a later invention. Not only were they published in the presence of friends and foes alike before the occurrence of their foretold events, but God Almighty has constituted another measure by which to establish the truth of their prior publication. Meaning to say, the Promised Messiah[as] lived under the authority of a government—the British—which professed a foreign religion and according to their regulations a copy of each and every book, periodical, essay or advertisement is filed with the [relevant] government department at the time of its publication. As a result, one can easily determine whether these prophecies were published beforehand by referring back to the official archives. This method of verification is one that cannot be controverted.

Thus in the face of such clear and insurmountable signs and proofs, how can one reject the claims of the Promised Messiah[as] and accept those of the previous prophets whose prophecies cannot be proven to have been published before the events they foretold, with the exception of the Holy Prophet[sa].

Further, one need not restrict themselves to those prophecies of the Promised Messiah[as] which relate to the past. Instead we observe that Allah the Exalted continues to show fresh signs in support of his truth. Only recently, two astonishing and powerful prophecies have been fulfilled, one pertaining to Mesopotamia and the other regarding the abdication of the Russian Tsar. I will deal with the former in a separate publication. In the current essay, it is this latter prophecy which I intend to set out before the world so that Allah the Exalted may enable pious souls to benefit from it.

As I have already mentioned the Promised Messiah[as] wrote a prophecy about the present war in an Urdu poem which included the following two lines:

مضمحل ہوجائیں گے اس خوف سے سب جن و انس

زار بھی ہو گا تو ہوگا اس گھڑی باحال زار

That is: 'Men high and low will be convulsed with fear and the Tsar himself will, at that hour, be in sad case.' This prophecy was recorded on 15 April 1905, in *Barahin-e-Ahmadiyya Part V*.[20] However, as can be seen from a supplementary note, for various reasons the book was not published until 1908. The prophecy was published again word for word, with an English translation in a 1914 edition of the *Review of Religions*.

[20] *Barahin-e-Ahmadiyya Part V*, *Ruhani Khaza'in* Vol. 21, p. 152 [Publishers]

An editorial note which accompanied the prophecy gave particular emphasis to this part of it. It said:

> The description is of a complex character and its dire details are dreadful enough to cause a shudder and make one's hair stand on end... But the name of [the] Russian Tsar attaches special interest to the predicted event.[21]

The prophecy was then republished in the [*Review of Religions*] of September 1914, June 1915 and January 1916. The prophecy was relayed in such clear terms that I need not go into a detailed explanation here. In plain words it stated that during the impending war, the Tsar of the Russian Empire would suffer a miserable plight and become an object of sympathy. In Urdu, the words used to express the condition of the Tsar are—حال زار (*haal-e-zaar*)—which mean to lose all of one's means and become so helpless that one's misery and ruin are obvious to see.

When this prophecy was first published, there was no indication of the events that have suddenly unfolded before us today in 1917. It is true that the Russians were at war with Japan, but [at the time of the prophecy] negotiations for peace had begun

[21] *Review of Religions,* August 1914, p. 307 [Publishers]

through the mediation of the Americans. Meanwhile the prophecy says: اک نشاں ہے آنیوالا آج سے کچھ دن کے بعد. That is: 'A sign will appear some days hence.' Meaning that a sign will appear after this date. Further it is clear that this calamity was to affect the whole world and cause widespread chaos. Thus the prophecy clearly distinguished the predicted events from the present and foretold a calamity which was going to afflict the world in the future. It was also set to be unlike anything the world had ever seen.

In summary, the prophecy was made at a time when it was impossible to know of these events through conjecture. It said that the Tsar would be reduced to ruin during an unprecedented calamity that would grip the whole world and:

خون سے مردوں کے کوہستان کے آب رواں

سرخ ہوجائیں گے جیسے ہو شراب انجبار

> The waters of mountain streams will run red like red wine; with the blood of the dead.

No such circumstances existed prior to 1914. Indeed, even the rulers of the aggressor nations did not initially foresee the dreadful course the [First World] War would take. Even certain British ministers said at the outbreak of hostilities that the war would be over by the end of the year and British soldiers would celebrate Christmas at home in the December of 1914. In light of this, the prophecy of 1905 was a mighty [sign] which vividly described the magnitude of the war and foretold that during the course of the conflict the Tsar would face a tragic plight and his circumstances would be made so pitiable and wretched that they would be clear for everyone to see. It is difficult to find a parallel to such a monumental prophecy in the history of the past prophets, and in view of the fact that there is historical evidence it was published before the time of its occurrence, its greatness is further enhanced.

The more one considers both the words of this prophecy and the supreme authority and influence held by the Tsar, and then further contemplates the circumstances under which he was forced to abdicate the crown and relinquish his power, the more the immensity and scope of the prophecy reveals itself. The extent of the sovereignty of the Tsar of Russia over his people is known to anyone who has studied Russian history. And as may be seen from a scholarly article in the Encyclopaedia Britannica under the heading of *Russia*, [prior to the fall of the Tsar], revolutionary elements in the country appeared to be moving towards a peaceful reconciliation and the administration of the Duma had done much to suppress any upheaval. Moreover, a regular Cossack militia, in whose loyalty the Tsar had complete confidence was ever present for his protection. And yet in spite of all this and the further subdual of rebel groups, the revolution which broke out on 12 March [1917] was so terrible that within three days the Tsar of Russia had been forced to abandon his throne. The graveness of the peril he faced can be seen from the constant fluctuations in his decision making. Initially, he informed his ministers that he was appointing General Alekseyev as the head of the government which shows how quickly the revolutionary movement had spread and how the Tsar, having been misinformed about the full extent of it at the beginning, considered it to be of little significance. Soon after, when he was told that the guards in the capital had revolted and the remaining imperial forces were joining the ranks of the revolutionaries, he resolved to abdicate in favour of his brother and when he saw that even this did not calm tensions, he made the following historic declaration:

> In agreement with the Duma we recognised that it was for the good of our country to abdicate the crown and lay down the supreme power.

But the tragedy of the Tsar did not end here. Following his abdication Russian officials placed him under arrest. According to a Reuters report:

> Prior to the ex-Tsar's arrival at Tsariskoe Selo delegates arrived at Magilev. They presented the mandate for the arrest of General Alexieff who informed the ex-Tsar who was waiting inside the imperial train.

What the ex-Tsar said in response to this forms a sad commentary on the prophecy: 'I am willing' said he 'to go anywhere and submit to any decision.' These words clearly indicate the helpless state of the Tsar. Again another report from Reuters describes the condition of the Tsar in the following terms:

> When he arrived at the imperial pavilion the ex-Tsar was wearing Cossack uniform. He stepped out calmly, but looked haggard and walked to the motor car.

A further Reuters report describes the condition of the Tsar after his arrest in even more wretched terms:

> They (newspapers) are publishing daily interviews with the Grand Duke revealing the

tragic isolation of the Tsar and Tsaritsa, who are wholly unacquainted with actualities in the country and the predictions of the Tsar's own family.

All of these details reveal how the ex-Tsar, who was once a powerful sovereign, was reduced to the helpless state of a pitiable creature and by this the following words of God Almighty were fulfilled:

زار بھی ہوگا تو ہوگا اس اس گھڑی باحال زار

The Tsar himself will, at that hour, be in sad case.

Besides the afore-detailed events, various other events from the Russian Revolution show that the Promised Messiah's[as] prophecy has been fulfilled in a truly remarkable manner.

First, as dispatches [coming out of the country] indicate, Russian thinkers of the day have concluded that there will no longer be a Tsar and instead the country is to be a republic. If the previous Tsar had been succeeded by another monarch, critics could have challenged the truth of the prophecy by arguing that one Tsar had been replaced by another who ruled in his stead in a far from wretched condition. However, the decision to form a republic means that the Tsardom has ended for good.

Secondly, the words of the prophecy indicated that the removal of the Tsar would happen in a manner other than through the murder of [Nichols II]; one who is killed cannot be said to suffer a pitiable plight. Misery can only accompany those who live and whose state of affairs so deteriorates that they are more helpless than their previous condition. And it was exactly such [a calamity] that overtook the Tsar. Instead of being executed [straight away], he was arrested and forced to abdicate and the entire world was witness to his unenviable end.

Thirdly, this prophecy was fulfilled in such a way that it is possible for us to freely publicise it and this in itself is proof of God Almighty's power. If the torment of the Tsar had been inflicted at the hands of the Germans or if the administration established after his abdication had not continued a cordial relationship with the British, the prevailing political climate would have prevented the publication of this prophecy. However, as prophecies such as this are meant for the guidance of people, God Almighty Himself brings about the means for their dissemination when they are finally fulfilled. With regards to the current prophecy, the overthrow of the Tsar did not occur in a manner which ran counter to the interests of the British government and, therefore, news of its fulfilment could be easily broadcast. This shows that the prophecy emanated from God Almighty Who not only foretold an event [of such momentous significance], but also brought about the means for its proclamation.

In closing, I call on people regardless of their religion, creed or country to consider whether or not this magnificent sign is ample proof that the person through whom it has been manifested is from God Almighty and from among those whom God sends. If not, then it will have to be conceded that the truth of any prophet cannot be verified.

My dear people, owing to the spread of iniquity and corruption, Allah the Exalted has willed to rehabilitate the world through truth and righteousness and to set it again on the path of virtue and piety. The mercy of our benevolent God, Who has always sent guides in times of disbelief and ever raised the sun of righteousness when darkness prevails, demands that the current age is not deprived of His compassion. Thus He has sent His messenger and opened the doors to His nearness. Let those whose hearts are filled with love and whose souls anxiously desire to prostrate before His threshold come forward, for the time of the fulfilment of God's desire has drawn close and the hour for the realization of His longing is at hand. Is not the fact that the followers of all religions are presently deprived of the supreme blessings which, by their own admission attended their forbears, enough to open the eyes of the wise. The followers of all faiths admit that their elders were recipients of divine revelation while they themselves are not. Are there no pious souls out there who would ponder why the door to revelation has been closed after having been open before? Surely this demonstrates that these religions have strayed from the guidance on which they were once set upon? How unfortunate that they blame God for these circumstances rather than confess their own shortcomings. They say God Almighty has closed the door to divine revelation without reason. People today act with the same piety as they did in the past, but God does not grant them the gift of revelation. However, they have failed to understand that God Almighty is ever ready to confer His bounties, and only their own abandonment of the path of divine pleasure has deprived them of these blessings. God speaks today just as He did before. He has spoken in this age to His Holiness, Mirza Ghulam Ahmad, the Promised Messiah[as] and indeed thousands of his followers.

People of India! Regardless of what community, religion or language group you belong to, I call on you to cherish that favour of God which He has bestowed upon you out of His Grace. For a prophet to come in any country is a source of great honour and is such a divine reward that nations yearn for it. Be glad that in this age God has chosen India, the country of your residence. People of various nations longed for this favour and all people desired that their country be chosen for this reward. But the grace of God chose India as the place for this favour. Thus, o' people of India no amount of rejoicing over this is sufficient. Can there be any greater foolishness than that God Almighty confers a reward on a country and its people choose to reject it? Therefore, hurry towards the truth for there you will find both worldly and religious honour. Those days are near when the name of India will be elevated through the Promised Messiah[as]. Indeed, they are so close at hand that the first light of dawn has broken. Thus do not be unmindful and do not be like a person in whose home there is a spring of water and people from all over set up camp around it and partake of its water, while he himself aches with thirst but does not try and drink from it. Fortunate souls from various countries are seizing the robe of the chosen one of God Almighty and thereby receiving spiritual blessings. So pity on this nation which despite being close is far away and despite being so near is remote and distant. The water of the Ganges is flowing in your homes. Bathe in its blessed water and cleanse yourself of your impurities, for in the sight of God it is not a person who washes himself in physical water who is clean, but rather one who purifies himself with the water of spirituality.

Again, I remind you o' people of India that to look after one's own honour is a natural inclination which is rooted in all human beings even if people differ in their level of merit. Numerous people unjustly ascribe all honourable things to their own person. One need only look at the state of the Muslims who have made replicas of gravestones or other such monuments which commemorate famous individuals throughout the world and then falsely claim that the replicas they have erected are in fact the authentic memorial. The same is true of the Hindus. There are numerous places which claim to be the place of birth or former place of residence of a past saint, because this elevates the honour of that site. When so much effort is made to acquire such false and fabricated honour, then why is true honour eschewed. Cherish the reward of God for this is for your betterment. If God has graced you with His favour this also brings with it great responsibility. The wrath of God strikes against those who reject His favours. Therefore, you must decide in your hearts whether the grace of God or His anger is more acceptable to you. Know well that no one has the strength to endure the wrath of God. Therefore, welcome His favour and bring faith in His avatar and chosen one to find peace both in this world and in the hereafter.

People of Europe and America! You have availed the material creation of God Almighty and greatly benefited from it and resultantly the secrets of the arts and sciences have been disclosed to you. Is this not then a sufficient incentive for you to explore the spiritual world so that you may achieve even greater success? Your own eyes are currently witness to the might of God Almighty. You are in a better position to recognise the gravity of the present World War and the pitiable plight of the Tsar than other people of the world. Profit from the signs of God Almighty so that you may become heirs to His grace. The Islam presented to you by the Christian clergy is a distortion and far removed from the truth. True Islam is a trove of abundant spiritual treasure as cannot be equalled by any other faith. [Jesus[as]] the Messiah once said that a tree is recognised by its fruit. Do not look at Islam from the perspective by which its enemies wish you to see it. Instead look at it from the perspective shown to you by the Messiah[as]. See for yourself how sweet are the fruits borne by Islam. At the present time there is no religion in the world capable of furnishing living proof of its truth except for Islam. It alone provides evidence of its life and only by following it can a person come to speak with God. So accept it and bring faith in that prophet (the Promised Messiah[as]) who attained his station from God through his complete loyalty to the Holy Prophet[sa] and by following the sharia of Islam. In this way you will be counted among those who follow all the commandments of God Almighty and accept all His prophets and the [resting] soul of [Jesus] the Messiah[as] will be pleased with you. For only those who truly accept [Jesus[as]] can also accept him who has come in his likeness. And those who reject the like of [Jesus[as]] also reject him in whose name he came.

وَاٰخِرُ دَعْوٰنَآ اَنِ الْحَمْدُ لِلّٰهِ رَبِّ الْعَالَمِيْنَ [22]

With Humility,
Mirza Mahmud Ahmad
Qadian, 4 April 1917

[22] And the conclusion of our prayer shall be, 'All praise be to Allah, the Lord of the worlds. [Publishers]

بِسۡمِ اللّٰہِ الرَّحۡمٰنِ الرَّحِیۡمِ نَحۡمَدُہٗ وَنُصَلِّیۡ عَلٰی رَسُوۡلِہِ الۡکَرِیۡمِ[23]

دنیا میں ایک نذیر آیا پر دنیا نے اس کو قبول نہ کیا۔ لیکن خدا اسے قبول کرے گا اور بڑے
زور آور حملوں سے اس کی سچائی ظاہر کر دے گا۔

A Warner came unto the world, but the world accepted him not; yet God shall manifest His favour and demonstrate his truth with powerful assaults.[24]

Signs of Divine Wrath

The day before yesterday that is on Wednesday, I received several critical and derisive tracts about the prophecy of the Promised Messiah[as] regarding the Tsar [of Russia].

As I read them, my heart was filled with sorrow at the sorry state of today's Muslims. Instead of rejoicing at the victory of Islam they are agonised by it; instead of enriching their faith they have chosen to move towards disbelief; and instead of recognising the chosen one of God they take pride in leading others astray.

Therefore, from the depths of my heart, I called on God to respond to the contentions of these naive souls

[23] In the name of Allah, the Gracious the Merciful. We praise Allah, the Exalted, the Greatest, and we invoke His blessings on His Holy Messenger[sa]. [Publishers]
[24] *Tadhkirah*, p. 128, 2009 Ed. [Publishers]

that they may be able to discern between what is good for them and what leads them to peril.

I am further astounded by the dishonesty of the author of these tracts who has made [every effort] to show that the severe calamity foretold by the Promised Messiah[as] referred to an earthquake and an earthquake alone. For this he cites the following reference from *Barahin-e-Ahmadiyya Part V*:

> Consider for yourself how this prophecy may be considered ambiguous when it clearly mentions an earthquake and says that a part of the country will be destroyed and also mentions that this will happen in my lifetime. (Page 90, line 9).[25]

In truth, the excerpt which he has quoted, does not refer to a future prophecy, rather it is a response to an individual who questioned how the earthquake of 4 April could be seen as a fulfilment of an earlier prophecy of the Promised Messiah[as]. Indeed, the second part of the question raised before the Promised Messiah[as] shows that the above passage was written in relation to this previous prophecy [and not the

[25] *Barahin-e-Ahmadiyya Part V*, *Ruhani Khaza'in* Vol. 21, p. 250-251 [Publishers]

prophecy regarding the Tsar].

The questioner writes to the Promised Messiah[as]:

> His holiness, Mirza Sahib has prophesied a second earthquake, but on this occasion he has also clarified that it has not been made known to him whether the impending calamity will come in the form of an earthquake or another severe catastrophe and nor has the time of its occurrence been made manifest. (Page. 91)

This clearly shows that the initial inquiry of the questioner was with regards to a previous earthquake which had already occurred [in accordance with the prophecy that foretold it], and the latter statement referred to a prophecy meant for the future. It is also clear that at the time of the second prophecy, the Promised Messiah[as] said it could signify a great calamity other than an earthquake. The answer given by the Promised Messiah[as] to the questioner also reveals this second prophecy did not necessarily foretell the coming of an earthquake, but could refer to another harrowing event. Further, the references cited by the author of the tract also indicate the Promised Messiah[as] himself suggested that the word *zalzala* could mean another catastrophe.

The following is one such reference from *Barahin-e-Ahmadiyya*:

> When and in which instance did I interpret the words of my prophecies to mean something other than an earthquake. Rather, I have always asserted that the primary and most common and predominant meaning of the word *zalzala* is an earthquake.

This shows the Promised Messiah[as] was open to the possibility that the word *zalzala* could signify another type of calamity. I will now present some further references in support of this claim.

On page 96 of the addendum of *Barahin-e-Ahmadiyya* the Promised Messiah[as] writes:

> I am quite amazed for I have said over and over again that in the first reckoning the word *zalzala* which appears in my prophecies refers to earthquakes. And if not, then it could denote another extraordinary catastrophe which bears close resemblance to an earthquake and possesses within it all of its characteristics. And yet despite this clarification such critics will not be satisfied.

Similarly, on page 120 of *Barahin-e-Ahmadiyya Part V* he says:

> It is possible that it may not be a common earthquake but some other dire calamity, which would be an example of the Judgment Day, the like of which has not been witnessed before, and which would bring about great destruction of life and property. [26]

After consulting these passages, any reasonable person can see the Promised Messiah[as] did not say for certain the prophesied calamity was a literal earthquake. Rather he always stipulated that it could be another ruinous misfortune which would devastate lives and property.

Now consider for a moment what type of calamity other than an earthquake itself would cause the destruction of both life and property while bearing similarity to this disaster. Is not the answer to this a war?

In the Holy Qur'an too, war has been likened to an earthquake. When Solomon[as] was set to attack Queen Sheba the Holy Qur'an quotes her as saying:

[26] *Barahin-e-Ahmadiyya Part V, Ruhani Khaza'in* Vol. 21, p. 151 [Publishers]

إِنَّ الْمُلُوكَ إِذَا دَخَلُوا قَرْيَةً أَفْسَدُوهَا وَجَعَلُوا أَعِزَّةَ أَهْلِهَا أَذِلَّةً[27]

That is, the obvious consequence of a war is that when a king enters another country as a victor, he turns the highest of its ranks into the lowest.

And this is how the Holy Qur'an describes the severity of earthquakes. With reference to the people of Lot it says:

جَعَلْنَا عَالِيَهَا سَافِلَهَا[28]

That is, the highest ranks were turned into the lowest. Hence war has a profound resemblance with earthquakes both in terms of its impact and the effect it has on different ranks of people. This is particularly true of modern warfare by which entire tunnels are blown away and the convulsions they cause resemble those of earthquakes.

His other objection that the Promised Messiah[sa] said the earthquake would strike in India and in his lifetime, stems from a lack of thought and reflection. With regards to the first contention, it ought to be clear the Promised Messiah[as] never said the earthquake

[27] 'Surely, kings, when they enter a country, despoil it, and turn the highest of its people into the lowest. *Surah An-Naml*, 27:35 [Publishers]
[28] *Surah Hud*, 11:83 [Publishers]

would not strike in another country. Rather he affirmed that this calamity would also occur in other places. He wrote:

> O' Europe, you are not secure; and O' Asia, you are not protected. O' ye that dwell in the islands, no artificial god will help you. I see cities falling and find the habitations in ruin.[29]

Similarly, the verses which contain the prophecy of the present war, clearly speak of a cataclysm of global proportions, as in the verse:

مضمحل ہو جائیں گے اس خوف سے سب جن و انس
زار بھی ہو گا تو ہو گا اس گھڑی باحال زار

> Men high and low will be convulsed with fear and the Tsar himself will, at that hour, be in sad case.[30]

Thus when the Promised Messiah[as] himself identifies the people of the world in general and the Tsar of Russia who lives over 7000 miles from India in particular as victims of this promised calamity, then to assert that the prophecy is undermined if the catastrophe occurs

[29] *Tadhkirah*, p. 881, 2009 Ed. [Publishers]
[30] *Tadhkirah*, p. 707, 2009 Ed. [Publishers]

anywhere outside of India is the height of ignorance. Such a contention would have carried some weight if India had been unaffected by the horrifying effects of this disaster. However, the thousands of native Indians who have been buried throughout the world in distant lands are testimony of the fact that India too bears the scars of this catastrophic war. If the author of this tract still harbours any doubt, he is free to visit the Punjab where every town and dwelling mourns the death of its loved ones who were slain by the bullets of the enemies of peace, and who spilled their blood like flowing water for their benevolent king and country. Indeed, he ought to speak to those distressed mothers, widows, orphaned children and elderly fathers who have had the apple of their eyes snatched away from them, who have lost the shade which sheltered them and the strength which supported them in their old age. He might then realise that now is the time for grief not ridicule and come to see how forcefully the word of God is fulfilled.

All that remains is to deal with the question of why the Promised Messiah[as] wrote that this calamity would appear in his lifetime. While this is certainly true, the perfect wisdom of God desired a different outcome and wanted for this disaster to strike not during the life of the Promised Messiah[as] but in the time of another promised individual. Therefore, Allah the Exalted taught him the following prayer through divine revelation:

رَبِّ اَخِّرْ وَقْتَ هٰذَا

> O' my God! Postpone the time of this earthquake which seems imminent.[31]

God Himself then gave the following answer for it:

اَخَّرَهُ اللّٰهُ اِلٰى وَقْتٍ مُّسَمًّى

That is, Allah the Exalted has postponed it until the appointed time.[32] This last revelation foretold that this particular earthquake would not occur during his life. However, it also revealed that it would strike within the limits of the appointed time, for Allah the Exalted said the calamity had been postponed and put back [not terminated indefinitely]. We can see the Promised Messiah[as] mentioned two things regarding the timing of the earthquake. First, it would occur in his lifetime and secondly it would strike within a period of 16 years.

[31] *Tadhkirah*, p. 808, 2009 Ed. [Publishers]
[32] *Tadhkirah*, p. 809, 2009 Ed. [Publishers]

Thus when divine revelation had revealed that though the disaster would not happen in the lifetime of the Promised Messiah[as], it would still occur within the stipulated time period, it was made clear that while the Promised Messiah[as] would not see it, it would still take place within 16 years. And this is exactly what happened. Ten years after the prophecy was made, it was fulfilled in the eleventh year.

It could be argued the fact that after receiving the revelations about an earthquake, the Promised Messiah[as] left his home and lived for some time in a tent shows he understood the word *zalzala* to mean an earthquake in a literal sense. However, such a contention would not be justified. Taking a precautionary measure in light of the presence of the word *zalzala* does not diminish the grandeur of the prophecy. It is often the practice of prophets to try and fulfil a prophecy in its literal sense and in the life of the Holy Prophet[sa], the incident of Hudaibiya is an example of this.

Also with regards to these revelations, it ought to be kept in mind the Promised Messiah[as] received numerous revelations about earthquakes; some of these revelations hinted at being fulfilled in his lifetime while others seemed to pertain to his homeland or to the rest of the world. In truth, it was not one earthquake that was prophesied but many.

God said to the Promised Messiah[as]: چمک دکھلاؤں گا تم کو اس نشاں کی پنج بار 'I shall show you the flash of this Sign five times.'[33] This revelation confirms that a wrathful sign would be forcefully manifested five times. Though other revelations spoke of the occurrence of various minor earthquakes, [in the revelation above] at least five were clearly mentioned. Consequently, two such earthquakes struck in the lifetime of the Promised Messiah[as] after this revelation; one in America and the other in Chile claiming the lives of 1500 and 2500 people respectively. The number of injured was even higher. Accordingly, many a person who sought the truth and was aware of these prophecies was guided by these events. Thus some of these earthquakes struck in his lifetime and steered people to the right path.

Another calamity, which was similar to an earthquake struck after the demise of Promised Messiah[as] in accordance with the revelation, and as the prophecy foretold, it affected the whole world, both the ruling classes and the general public. This grievous torment had particular impact on Europe and the Tsar of Russia. Again, these signs gave guidance to many

[33] *Tadhkirah*, p. 804, 2009 Ed. [Publishers]

people, but those who are eternally blind cannot hope to see the light of the sun of spirituality. They are [as the Persian proverb suggests] like dogs that bark at those who spread light. Such people ought to bear in mind that it is not beyond the might of God to cause earthquakes to happen. I received a pamphlet today which ridiculed this prophecy and my heart grieved as I read it. A violent tremor hit that very night and though many of the details are still unclear, reports suggest a large earthquake caused this. According to some, the shocks were more horrifying than the ones from the previous earthquake which struck [Kangra] on April 4, 1905. A resident of Dharamsala wrote:

> Tonight at 3:17am, a powerful earthquake struck the earth. The ground shook violently for almost half a minute and caused most of the shops and houses to collapse. In Tika Chola all of the houses were ruined and in Bagicha Toa, one man was killed as his home collapsed on him while a number of others sustained injuries.

> He further writes:

> This earthquake was more severe than the one which struck [Kangra] on April 4, 1905.

As of now the circumstances are still unclear and we will only know the exact picture once the full details have emerged. However, what we know so far ought to be sufficient to open the eyes of the ignorant. There are two signs in this. First, through the fulfilment of the prophecy of the Promised Messiah[as] frequent earthquakes were to occur. Secondly, God fulfilled this prophecy immediately as a rebuke to certain foul-mouthed enemies and effectively said to them:

> Foolish people, I can cause earthquakes as well. If the people of this country will cease in their brazenness only after being jolted by earthquakes then I am ready for this.

Do not think earthquakes are just a natural occurrence. Such an approach is dangerous and has caused the ruin of many nations. Allah says:

وَمَآ اَرْسَلْنَا فِيْ قَرْيَةٍ مِّنْ نَّبِيٍّ اِلَّآ اَخَذْنَآ اَهْلَهَا بِالْبَاْسَآءِ وَالضَّرَّآءِ لَعَلَّهُمْ
يَضَّرَّعُوْنَ ○ ثُمَّ بَدَّلْنَا مَكَانَ السَّيِّئَةِ الْحَسَنَةَ حَتّٰى عَفَوْا وَّقَالُوْا قَدْ مَسَّ
اٰبَآءَنَا الضَّرَّآءُ وَالسَّرَّآءُ فَاَخَذْنٰهُمْ بَغْتَةً وَّهُمْ لَا يَشْعُرُوْنَ ○[34]

> And never did We send a Prophet to any town but We seized the people thereof with adversity

[34] *Surah Al-A'raf*, 7:95-96 [Publishers]

and suffering, that they might become humble. Then We changed *their* evil *condition* into good until they grew *in affluence and number* and said, 'Suffering and happiness betided our fathers *also*.' Then We seized them suddenly, while they perceived not.

Hence, such a way of thought is fatal and is entertained by those who stray away from certainty. In truth, calamities only strike when God has raised a messenger. Allah the Exalted says:

وَمَا كُنَّا مُعَذِّبِيْنَ حَتّٰى نَبْعَثَ رَسُوْلًا[35]

We never punish until We have sent a Messenger.

Do not consider the punishment of God a small or trivial thing. Instead it serves as a sign that a prophet of God has been raised in this time. Let those who have eyes see and let those who have ears listen that the current series of earthquakes is not usual or ordinary. Instead, they are unmatched by the earthquakes of the past, both in number and severity. The Promised Messiah[as] writes in *Barahin-e-Ahmadiyya*:

[35] *Surah Bani Isra'il*, 17:16 [Publishers]

دنیا میں ایک نذیر آیا پر دنیا نے اس کو قبول نہ کیا۔ لیکن خدا اُسے قبول
کرے گا اور بڑے زور آور حملوں سے اُس کی سچائی ظاہر کر دے گا۔

A Warner came unto the world, but the world accepted him not; yet God shall manifest His favour and demonstrate his truth with powerful assaults.

اَلْفِتْنَةُ هٰهُنَا فَاصْبِرْ كَمَا صَبَرَ اُولُوا الْعَزْمِ فَلَمَّا تَجَلّٰى رَبُّهٗ لِلْجَبَلِ
جَعَلَهٗ دَكًّا قُوَّةُ الرَّحْمٰنِ لِعُبَيْدِ اللّٰهِ الصَّمَدِ

There is a trail here, then be steadfast as were the Prophets of high resolve. When the Lord will manifest Himself on the mountain of difficulties, He will crush them into bits. It is the power of the Gracious God, which He, the Independent and Besought of all, will demonstrate for His servant.[36]

Even if we ignore other natural disasters, the sheer number of recent earthquakes is sufficient evidence [of the fulfilment of this prophecy] for those who would perceive. Encyclopaedic records account for the deadliest earthquakes in the world over the past three centuries, along with the number of casualties.

36 *Tadhkirah*, p. 129, 2009 Ed. [Publishers]

From this it can be seen that these disasters paled into insignificance when compared to the ones under present discussion. Here I have divided them into two periods, that is the time before the publication of *Barahin-e-Ahmadiyya* and the time after. This is sufficient to show that over this short period of time, earthquakes have increased exponentially and caused grave losses. They, therefore, provide a stark contrast with what passed before. The following table is a list of earthquakes that occurred before the publication of *Barahin*:

Location	Number of Fatalities	Year
Sicily	60,000	1693
Lima	18,000	1724
Aleppo	22,000	1822
Calabria	10,000	1857
Lisbon	50,000	1755
Calabria	60,000	1783
Kyoto	41,000	1797
Caracas	12,000	
Mendoza	12,000	1860
Peru and Ecuador	25,000	1868
Manila	3000	1880

[Here is a list of earthquakes] after *Barahin-e-Ahmadiyya* was published:

Location	Number of Fatalities	Year
Ischia	2000	1883
Krakatoa	35,000	1883
Japan	26,000	1896
Mount Pelee	20,000	1902
India	15,000	1905
San Francisco	1500	1906
Valparaiso, Chile	2500	1906
Jamaica	1000	1907
Messina and Calabria	300,000	1908

According to these figures, in the first recorded 290 years the death toll from 11 earthquakes stood at 313,000 lives. However, in the 10 earthquakes that have occurred over the past 26 years, the number of fatalities is documented at 403,000 an increase of almost 100,000 indicating that earthquakes have become deadlier. Two further earthquakes which struck in Italy and Turkey in 1914 increase the number of earthquakes and add another 100,000 to the death toll. It is important to note that the number of people who have died from earthquakes since the revelation of the Promised Messiah[as] is more than the last 300 years combined and multiple earthquakes have occurred over a short period of time. It is also worth noting that after the revelation of the Promised Messiah[as] foretelling the impending onset of earthquakes, such disasters occurred for four years straight, in 1905, '06, '07 and '08. The number of deaths in these four years is also in excess of the previous 300 years in which 313,000 people lost their lives. In contrast, over these four years, 7000 additional deaths occurred after the Promised Messiah[as] had prophesied this calamity. *Take heed, o' you who would understand.*

Finally, I call on all those who seek the truth to have mercy on their lives and wealth. Refrain from abusing the messenger of God. Remember well, the jealous regard Allah shows [for His loved ones]. There is no one who can compete with Him. He has shown hundreds of thousands of signs in support of the Promised Messiah[as] which were acknowledged by both his enemies and the liberal minds of Europe. Why do you bring misfortune on yourself and deprive yourself of those divine blessings which people from far flung places have accepted? I call on those who identify themselves as Muslims and who assert love for the Holy Prophet[sa], to fear God and refrain from challenging the khalifa and representative of the Holy Prophet[sa] and ask them whether they will come face to face with the Holy Prophet[sa] on the Day of Judgment? Do they not wish to see the triumph and glory of Islam? If so, why do you seethe at the time of Islam's victory just because it establishes the truth of Hazrat Mirza Ghulam Ahmad[as]? He has not done you any such wrong that you should allow yourself to tolerate the abuse of both Islam and the Holy Prophet[sa] out of enmity to him. Know that God is true to His promise. The sun has risen. Darkness will now dwell in derelict buildings, tight hollows and caves. Think not that the efforts of anyone can destroy or bring harm to this community. Its truthfulness will most certainly spread and be broadcast throughout all the countries of the world. Recognise this moment and have mercy on Islam. Rather, have mercy on your souls, and hasten to accept the truth which promises to raise your honour and to deliver victory to Islam over the other religions of the world through irrefutable proofs and arguments.

وَاٰخِرُ دَعْوَانَآ اَنِ الْحَمْدُ لِلّٰهِ رَبِّ الْعٰلَمِيْنَ [37]

[37] And the conclusion of our prayer shall be, 'All praise be to Allah, the

With Humility,
Mirza Mahmud Ahmad
Khalifatul-Masih II
Qadian Darul-Aman, District Gurdaspur
12 May 1917

Lord of the worlds. [Publishers]

Glossary

Hadith or *Ḥadīth* (حَدِيث) the recorded sayings and traditions of the Holy Prophet[sa].

Hazrat or *Ḥaḍrat* (حَضرت) an honorific Arabic title.

Khalifa or *Khalīfah* (خَلِيْفه) term used for Islamic spiritual leaders, particularly the successors of the Holy Prophet[sa] and the Promised Messiah[as].

Khalifatul Masih or *Khalīfatul Masīḥ* (خَلِيْفَةُ الْمَسِيْح) title conferred on the spiritual successors of the Promised Messiah[as].

Kishti or *Kishtī* (کشتی) boat or ship.

Sharia or *Sharī'ah* (شريعه) literally *path* or *way*. The word sharia is often used with reference to Islamic law or the various duties and obligations of Muslims.

Zalzala or *Zalzalah* (زلزله) an earthquake.